A Son is Given

Burl L. Shepard

© 2021 by Burl L. Shepard. All rights reserved.

Words Matter Publishing
P.O. Box 531
Salem, Il 62881
www.wordsmatterpublishing.com

No part of this publication may be reproduced, stored in a retrieval system, or transmitted in any way by any means—electronic, mechanical, photocopy, recording, or otherwise—without the prior permission of the copyright holder, except as provided by USA copyright law.

ISBN 13: 978-1-953912-22-0

Library of Congress Catalog Card Number: 2021941555

Dedication

This is dedicated to my late sister, Margie.
She is more than a memory, for she is now
basking in the glory of God.

"Now we see but a poor reflection as in a mirror;
then we shall see face to face.
Now I know in part;
then I shall know fully,
even as I am fully known.

And now these three remain;
faith hope and love.
But the greatest of these is love"
(1 Corinthians 13:12-13 NIV).

TABLE OF CONTENTS

The Trinity 1

Who Did He Think He Was? 5

The Lord's Prayer 9

Words That Would Change Our Country 11

Saul to Paul—A Different Man 15

The Ten Commandments Exodus 20:3-17 NIV 25

Controlling the Tongue 33

The Parable of the Rich Fool 35

A Child is Born A Son is Given 41

Beautiful Words, Wonderful Promise,
Dreadful Warning, Wisdom Speaks 43

The Unforgivable Sin 47

A Son is Given

IS THERE A sovereign God who created everything seen and unseen, who sees all, knows all, and controls all? Or did a bolt of lightning striking a muddy pool of water millions of years ago start a chain of events that has led to what exists today? This is a question everyone must answer for themselves.

Without God and his moral code, good and evil do not exist. There is nothing upon which to draw other than self, for without good there cannot be evil, and without evil, there cannot be good. There is nothing but a void, without content, and from that void, every individual must establish their own doctrine of morals.

A dictator might cause thousands of deaths and unbelievable suffering through any means they thought was necessary in order to hold onto power. No matter how society as a whole might regard it, it would not be wrong, for the dictator drew upon the void without content, and was smart enough to make it happen. The situation would be right until someone who was smarter and stronger appeared on the scene, who drew differently from the void without content, and then what was right would change.

No matter what was done in secret, no matter how terrible or perverse some might consider the acts to be, or how much harm was done to innocent people including children, it would not be wrong, for again, the acts were drawn from the void without content, neither good nor evil.

I'm open to both the biblical account of creation as well as the possibility of God-controlled evolution. My concern is not how God brought everything into being, but that God did bring everything into being. But, if life started neither from the biblical account of creation or God-controlled evolution, somebody please tell me where the bolt of lightning and puddle of water came from?

Filter or transmission theories of the mind (James 1898-1900; Schiller, 1891-1894) according to which mind is not generated by the brain but instead focused, limited and constrained by it. Irreducible Mind Page XXX Introduction.

We are both physical and spiritual beings. The physical brain acts as a filter that prevents us from receiving spiritual information that would not allow us to live our physical lives. When what we think of as death occurs and the physical brain dies, the spiritual mind is immediately freed from all restraints and we enter the spiritual realm. Death is not the end, but the beginning of life; it is the beginning of life the way it was meant to be for those who believe.

The Trinity

THE FATHER, THE Son, and the Holy Spirit exist together as one but at the same time exist as separate entities, each in their own way as significant as the other two. How is it possible for there to be one and yet three at the same time? Consider this:

Picture a room fourteen feet in length, fourteen feet in width, and fourteen feet in height. Imagine this room to be the universe. In the center of the room, on the ceiling, is a porcelain light fixture. This is the throne of God and is at the highest point in the universe. In the porcelain light fixture, there is a 100-watt, old-fashioned incandescent light bulb. Imagine the lightbulb is God the Father on his throne with the earth as his footstool. Turn the bulb on and the room is instantly filled with light. The light coming from the bulb is God the Son, continually existing with the bulb while at the same time going out from the bulb, lighting the room, and continually existing apart from the bulb. Now, take your hand and place it close to the bulb. Don't touch the bulb for the incandescent bulbs get hot. The warmth coming from the bulb is God the Holy Spirit, continually existing with the bulb while at the same time going out from the bulb and continually existing apart from the bulb.

"Since ancient times no one has heard, no ear has perceived, no eyes have seen any God besides you, who acts on behalf of those who wait for him" (Isaiah 64:4 NIV). — God the Father

"He is the image of the invisible God, the firstborn over all creation. For by him all things were created" (Colossians 1:15-16 NIV). — God the Son

"The Son is the radiance of God's glory and the exact representation of his being, sustaining all things by his powerful word" (Hebrews 1:3 NIV). — God the Son

"I and the father are one" (John 10:30 NIV). — God the Son

"If you love me, you will obey what I command. And I will ask the Father, and He will give you another counselor to be with you forever, the Spirit of Truth" (John 14:15-16 NIV). — God the Holy Spirit

"In the beginning, God created the heavens and the earth. Now the earth was formless and empty, darkness was over the surface of the deep, and the spirit of God was hovering over the waters" (Genesis 1:1-2 NIV). — God the Holy Spirit

Why do bad, even terrible things happen to good, sometimes innocent people? How could a God of love and forgiveness allow for that?

We live in a fallen world, a world in which God has

established physical laws. However, we are both physical and spiritual beings. We are spiritual beings that for an incredibly short period of time when compared to eternity, are contained within a physical body. Whether we are good people, bad people, followers of God, nonbelievers, or children, while within the physical body, we must abide by God's physical laws.

Imagine two followers of Christ, their child, and a nonbeliever standing at the base of a brick building. A small tremor occurs, strong enough to cause loose bricks to break loose from the building and fall on the people below. Tragically, all four are killed. It might be asked, how could a loving God allow this to happen, especially to his two followers and their innocent child? It happened because of the effect caused by God's physical laws.

God could have intervened and saved all or any of the four people. He is in control of the laws he has established, both physical and spiritual. If he had intervened in regard to any of the four people, it would have been because their appointed time had not yet come, the reason known only to God. In that case, he would have performed a miracle, something he does quite well.

If there had not been a reason for a miracle in regard to any of the four, when their physical bodies and brains died, their spiritual minds would have been freed from their physical bodies. The two believers and their child would have stood before God before entering into eternal life. The nonbeliever would have stood before God for judgment.

God created science; science is not our God. Do not rely on the fixed physical laws God created in searching for life's meaning. Turn to the creator himself. Only then will you find meaning in life

"The Lord is my shepherd, I shall not be in want. He makes me lie down in green pastures, he leads me beside quiet waters, he restores my soul. He guides me in paths of righteousness for his name's sake. Even though I walk through the valley of the shadow of death, I will fear no evil, for you are with me; your rod and your staff, they comfort me. You prepare a table before me in the presence of my enemies. You anoint my head with oil; my cup overflows. Surely goodness and love will follow me all the days of my life, and I will dwell in the house of the Lord forever" (Psalm 23 NIV).

Taken from Psalm 23

He will guide your way and provide for your needs. He will give you rest, peace, and replenish your soul. He will direct your paths for his glory. He will protect you through the valleys of despair. He will always be with you. He will give you strength in the presence of those who would do you harm. Your head held high, he will provide more than enough. His presence and power will be with you during your journey through the physical realm, and you will then be with him in the spiritual realm forever.

Who Did He Think He Was?

BESIDES THE TWELVE disciples, Jesus appointed seventy-two others to go ahead of him to places he was about to go. (Luke 1 NIV) When they returned, they were overwhelmed by the things they were able to do in his name. He then made three amazing statements: "I saw Satan fall like lightning from heaven. I have given you authority to trample on snakes and scorpions and to overcome all the power of the enemy; nothing will harm you. However, do not rejoice that the spirits submit to you, but rejoice that your names are written in heaven" (Luke 10:18-20 NIV).

1. Jesus said he was there during the war in heaven when Michael and his angels fought Satan and his angels and Satan was hurled to the earth and his angels with him (Revelation 12:7-9 NIV).

2. He said he had authority over the demons and through his power his followers would not be harmed.

3. Then, he had the audacity to say he knew whose names were written in the Book of Life.

Who did this man think he was, God?

"And there was war in heaven. Michael and his angels fought against the dragon, and the dragon and his angels fought back. But he was not strong enough, and they lost their place in heaven. The great dragon was hurled down—that ancient serpent called the devil, or Satan, who leads the whole world astray. He was hurled to the earth, and his angels with him" (Revelation 12:7-9 NIV).

"Therefore rejoice, you heavens and you who dwell in them! But woe to the earth and the sea, because the devil has gone down to you! He is filled with fury because he knows that his time is short" (Revelation 12:12 NIV).

The battle of all battles: when Satan and his followers rebelled against God and were cast from heaven. The heavens rejoiced, but the earth was cursed by him who is now in the world. Satan uses any means possible to separate humankind from God but realizes he will be the ultimate loser in the ongoing spiritual warfare.

Once, when the angels presented themselves before God, Satan also came with them. God asked Satan what he had been doing. Satan replied, "From roaming through the earth and going back and forth in it" (Job 1:6-7 NIV).

Why was Satan roaming throughout the earth? He was doing what he always does, looking for victims, trying to draw them from God and into the evilness of the world.

For Satan himself masquerades as an angel of light. It is not surprising then that his servants masquerade as servants of righteousness. Their end will be what their actions deserve" (2 Corinthians 11:14-15 NIV).

Satan sometimes removes his cloak of darkness, taking the appearance of an angel in order to deceive. Likewise, there are those who claim to be followers of Christ, whose only interests are personal gain and living according to he who is in the world.

"But the Lord is faithful, and he will strengthen and protect you from the evil one" (2 Thessalonians 3:3 NIV).

"You dear children are from God and have overcome them, because the one who is in you is greater than the one who is in the world" (1 John 4:4 NIV).

The power of God. It begins as a thought. Could it possibly be true? During this period, it is me, the devil, and maybe God. As time passes, so do inner feelings. Then, it is me, the devil, and God. More time passes. I've learned more about God and his ways. I find it is now me, God, and the devil. Suddenly, to my astonishment, it is God, me, and the devil. And then, only on rare occasions do I feel Satan's evil presence. But he cannot gain entry, for now it is God and me. As God moves in, the devil moves out.

The Lord's Prayer

"**OUR FATHER WHICH** art in heaven, Hallowed be thy name, Thy kingdom come, Thy will be done in earth as it is in heaven, Give us this day our daily bread: And forgive us our trespasses, As we forgive them that trespass against us: And lead us not into temptation, But deliver us from evil. For thine is the kingdom, the power, and the glory, For ever and ever. Amen."

(Source: The Litany section of the US Book of Common Prayer, 1925 edition.

Taken from the Lord's Prayer

WORDS THAT WOULD CHANGE OUR COUNTRY

"**DO NOTHING OUT** of selfish ambition or vain conceit, but in humility consider others better than yourselves. Each of you should look not only to your own interest, but also to the interest of others" (Philippians 2:3-4 NIV).

If followed, these are the words that would change this country. But could it ever happen? For example, think of these words in the context of politics. It's laughable to believe politicians would ever abide by them. What about other areas of society, what about our institutions, our places of business, places of worship, sports and other areas of entertainment, and yes, family units as well as those who are single? It will happen, not just in this country, but throughout the world. But it won't happen until Jesus returns.

God— Sex

"The man said, 'This is now bone of my bones and flesh of my flesh; she shall be called woman, for she was taken out of man.'

For this reason a man will leave his father and mother and be united to his wife, and they will become one flesh" (Genesis 2:23-24 NIV).

Sex is a God-given gift of intimacy between one man and one woman during which you are sharing as much of your being as possible with your spouse. However, after the fall, because of Satan's rule, many times sex becomes perverted and is not used as God intended. When this happens, it has no meaning but many adverse repercussions.

Satan—Sex

Adultery can cause heartache and unbearable emotional stress. Families are torn apart. Relationships are ended forever. Also, some people married and unmarried choose multiple sex partners. It has been said that whenever you have sex with someone, you are also having sex with every other sex partner that person has ever been with. This is something that often causes a chain reaction of disease among many people, sometimes occurring many years after the encounters happened and even ending in death. And of course, there is always unwanted pregnancy. Satan looks on with glee.

Abortion—Life in the Womb

In an account of a rally for the right to choose movement, I heard of some young women referring to the unborn fetus as a parasite. This is a statement that should bring tears to the eyes. Consider the word of God.

"For you created my inmost being, you knit me together in my mother's womb" (Psalm 139:13 NIV).

"My frame was not hidden from you when I was made in the secret place" (Psalm 139:15 NIV).

"Your eyes saw my unformed body. All the days ordained for me were written in your book befor one of them came to be" (Psalm 139:16 NIV).

"This is what the Lord says — he who made you, who formed you in the womb, and who will help you, 'do not be afraid,' "(Isaiah 44:2 NIV).

Countless souls have been taken to heaven prematurely because of the sin of abortion. But, consider this: "The Lord will fulfill his purpose for me, your love, oh Lord endures forever — do not abandon the works of your hands" (Psalm 138:8 NIV).

The Lord will fulfill his purpose, his love does last forever, and he will not abandon the works of his hands for there is a special place in heaven for those who have been stolen from their mother's womb's.

Saul to Paul—A Different Man

PAUL'S TEACHINGS ARE the foundation for finding the way to salvation. Much of the New Testament was written by him. We must believe his writings in order to find the faith we need.

He had an encounter with Jesus while traveling to Damascus (Acts 9:3-6 NIV) and after reaching Damascus, was filled with the Holy Spirit (Acts 8:17-19 NIV).

In 2 Corinthians 12:1-4 (NIV), Paul talks about what today might be called an out-of-body experience in which he heard inexpressible things; things that man is not permitted to tell.

This man, who was at first called Saul, was completely changed by his encounter with Christ in a way so dramatic he was given a different name, for he was indeed a different person. Paul knew the importance of forgetting the past, and he had much to forget for in his old life as Saul, he had been responsible for the deaths of many believers.

He writes, "But one thing I do: Forgetting what is behind and straining toward what is ahead, I press on toward the goal to win the prize for which God has called me heavenward in Christ Jesus" (Philippians 3:13-14 NIV).

We can believe these words are true when he writes: "I want you to know, brothers, that the gospel I preached is not something that man made up. I did not receive it from any man, nor was I taught it; rather I received it by revelation from Jesus Christ" (Galatians 1:11-12 NIV).

"All Scripture is God-breathed" (2 Timothy 3:16 NIV).

The Holy Bible is God's Word. It speaks to us all, sometimes in different ways. There have been atheists who have researched the Bible for the sole purpose of discrediting it but within its pages found the true meaning of life which resulted in them becoming followers of Christ. The Bible fills the void we have if we have no moral authority showing us what is good and what is evil.

"All men are like grass, and all their glory is like the flowers of the field; the grass withers and the flowers fall, but the word of the Lord stands forever" (1 Peter 1:24-25 NIV).

Take God out of the equation, and the truth of the remainder of the statement cannot be denied. Whether it's an early death due to sickness or accident, or after a long life, productive or not, no matter what our accomplishments, we all will die. Without God, all that remains is stark emptiness.

"Since the children have flesh and blood, he too shared in their humanity so that by his death he might destroy him who holds the power of death—that is the devil—and free those who all their lives were held in slavery by their fear of death" (Hebrews 2:14-15 NIV).

The death of Jesus on the cross eliminated the natural inherent fear of death for all who accept him as Savior and Lord. The emptiness is gone.

"Do not let your hearts be troubled. Trust in God, trust also in me" (John 14:1 NIV).

"I will lie down and sleep in peace, for you alone, O Lord, make me dwell in safety (Psalm 4:8 NIV).

Only faith in what Jesus did on the cross can give true peace and comfort.

"My soul finds rest in God alone; my salvation comes from him. He alone is my rock and my salvation; He is my fortress; I will never be shaken" (Psalm 62:1-2 NIV).

"Be joyful in hope, patient in affliction, faithful in prayer" (Romans 12:12 NIV).

"In the beginning was the word, and the Word was with God and the Word was God. He was with God in the beginning. Through him all things were made; without him, nothing was made that has been made. In him was life, and that life was the light of men. The light shines in the darkness, but the darkness has not understood it" (John 1:1-5 NIV).

"He is the image of the invisible God, the firstborn over all creation. For by him all things were created: things in heaven and on earth, visible and invisible, whether thrones or powers or rulers or authorities, all things were created by him and for him. He is before all things, and in him all things hold together" (Colossians 1:15-17 NIV).

Everything that was made, seen and unseen, was made by him. He was life for mankind. Everything exists through him. The powers of darkness cannot understand his love.

"Why, you do not even know what will happen tomorrow. What is your life? You are a mist that appears for a little while and then vanishes" (James 4:14 NIV).

Walk up to a solid wall. Stop about three feet from it. What do you notice as you look at the wall? You will notice the color and probably whatever designs that might be in the wall. However, you cannot see what is beyond the wall. Likewise, we all have a permanent wall between ourselves and whatever remains of our physical lives. God's appointed time for us and what lies beyond the physical realm could occur at any moment.

"I am the light of the world. Whoever follows me will never walk in darkness, but will have the light of life" (John 8:12 NIV).

"But I, when I am lifted up from the earth, will draw all men to myself" (John 12:32 NIV).

Jesus told his followers the way he was going to die. None of them could ever have imagined how his crucifixion would over the centuries draw people to him from throughout the world, and this will continue to happen until he returns.

"But now I have chosen Jerusalem for my name to be

there, and I have chosen David to rule my people Israel" (2 Chronicles 6:6 NIV).

Israel was formed as a Jewish state in 1948. Jerusalem is now its capital. Over the centuries, all divinely inspired predictions concerning Israel have come to pass. All is moving along according to God's timetable.

"'For I know the plans I have for you,' declares the Lord, 'plans to prosper you and not to harm you, plans to give you hope and a future' " (Jeremiah 29:11 NIV).

"I will bless those who bless you and whoever curses you I will curse" (Genesis 12:3 NIV).

"Blessed is the nation whose god is the Lord" (Psalm 33:12 NIV).

If America turns away from the principles established by the founding fathers, God will turn away from America. John Adams wrote, "Our constitution was made only for a religious and moral people. It is wholly inadequate for the government of any other."

America has been blessed because of its close ties with and backing of Israel. However, there are many in America who wish to sever those ties. It would be a terrible mistake to betray God's chosen people for that would result in God turning away from America.

"I swear by myself, declares the Lord, that because you have done this and have not withheld your son, your only son, I will surely bless you and make your descendants as numerous as the stars in the sky and as the sand on the seashore. Your descendants will take possession of the cities of their enemies, and through your offspring all nations on earth will be blessed, because you have obeyed me" Genesis 22:16-18 NIV).

If in fact Abraham was justified by works, he had something to boast about—but not before God. What does the scripture say? Abraham believed God and it was credited to him as righteousness" (Romans 4:2-3 NIV).

Abraham believed and showed trust in God after God tested him by telling him to sacrifice his son Isaac. When Abraham started to carry out the command, the angel of the Lord called out from heaven for him not to harm his son. The fact that Abraham was going to obey this command was credited to him as being righteous. This righteousness was not through obeying the law which was not in effect at the time, but through the righteousness that comes by faith. The promise that Abraham would be heir of the world came by his faith so that it would be grace and that righteousness by grace instead of trying to obey the law would be guaranteed to all who would ask. Abraham is the father of all believers.

"So do not fear, for I am with you; do not be dismayed, for I am your God: I will strengthen you and help you; I will uphold you with my righteous right hand" (Isaiah 41:10 NIV).

As God will help Israel, so will he help all Gentiles who believe, for through their faith they also are children of Abraham.

In regard to Israel, God has been compared to a jealous lover. That small Jewish nation will continue to be the focal point of many meaningful world events.

"Be careful not to forget the covenant of the Lord your God that he made with you; do not make for yourselves an idol in the form of anything the Lord your God has forbidden. For the Lord your God is a consuming fire, a jealous God" (Deuteronomy 4:23-24 NIV).

"This is what the Lord Almighty says: 'I am very jealous for Zion; I am burning with jealousy for her' " (Zechariah 8:2 NIV).

"A man's steps are directed by the Lord. How can anyone understand his own way?" (Proverbs 20:24 NIV).

"Trust the Lord with all your heart and lean not on your own understanding; in all your ways acknowledge him, and he will make your paths straight" (Proverbs 3:5-6 NIV).

Speak to God about everything. Then, listen for His voice. He will guide you through all aspects of your life.

"Therefore, I tell you whatever you ask for in prayer, believe that you have received it, and it will be 'yours" (Mark 11:24 NIV).

What we think we need, and what God knows we need, could be at odds with each other. Our prayers will be answered, but in accordance with the Holy Spirit who prays for us and knows what our future holds.

"Unless the Lord builds the house, its builders labor in vain, unless the Lord watches over the city, the watchmen stand guard in vain" (Psalms 127:1 NIV).

Without God's help, the foundations of all endeavors

can easily crumble. Without God's protection, no fortification is truly secure.

"The fear of the Lord—that is wisdom, and to shun evil is understanding" (Job 28:28 NIV).

It has been said, in regard to God, the word fear means showing deep respect. But Jesus said to not fear those who threaten and kill the body and then can do no more, but to fear him who holds your entire being in his hands (Luke 12:4-5 NIV). In some ways, the awesome power of God and the finality he could bring deserve more than respect.

"The heavens declare the glory of God; the skies proclaim the works of his hands. Day after day they pour forth speech; night after night they display knowledge. There is no speech or language where their voice is not heard. Their voice goes out into all the earth, their words to the end of the world" (Psalms 19:1-4 NIV).

"I devoted myself to study and to explore by wisdom all that is done under heaven. What a heavy burden God has laid on men! I have seen all of the things that are done under the sun; all of them are meaningless, a chasing after the wind" (Ecclesiastes 1:13-14 NIV).

When King Solomon made this unprecedented remark, he was not looking above the sun into the spiritual realm of God which is forever and where true meaning can be found but at the world below where our journey is but a short while with no lasting effect..

"As you do not know the path of the wind, or how the body is formed in a mother's womb, so you cannot understand the work of God, the maker of all things" (Ecclesiastes 11:5 NIV).

Often, thousands of people flee large populated areas due to an approaching hurricane. Sometimes, thankfully they return to a landscape that is unchanged because the path of the storm changed. On a more tragic note, firefighters in rough forested terrain have lost their lives due to a sudden shift of the wind. Also, the wonderment of the human body cannot be fully explained. As we cannot fully understand nature or even ourselves, we will never fully understand God's ways.

"Nothing in all creation is hidden from God's sight. Everything is uncovered and laid bare before the eyes of him to whom we must give account" (Hebrews 4:13 NIV).

"For God will bring every deed into judgement, including every hidden thing, whether it is good or evil" (Ecclesiastes 12:14 NIV).

"For a man's ways are in full view of the Lord, and he examines all his paths" (Proverbs 5:21 NIV).

This should be a disturbing matter to consider. God knows everything you have ever done or thought, and will know everything you do or think from this moment forward.

"A gentle answer turns away wrath, but a harsh word stirs up anger" (Proverbs 15:1 NIV).

How easily anger flares when we disagree. This is a common-sense approach for a civil discussion.

The Ten Commandments
Exodus 20:3-17 NIV

- "You shall have no other gods before me.
- You shall not make for yourself an idol in the form of anything.
- You shall not misuse the name of the Lord your God.
- Remember the Sabbath day by keeping it holy.
- Honor your father and your mother.
- You shall not murder.
- You shall not commit adultery.
- You shall not steal.
- You shall not give false testimony.
- You shall not covet."

"BUT IN THE account of the bush, even Moses showed that the dead rise, for he calls the Lord the God of Abraham, and the God of Isaac, and the God of Jacob. He is not the God of the dead, but of the living, for to him, all are alive" (Luke 20:37-38 NIV).

"I am the resurrection and the life. He who believes in me will live, even though he dies; and whoever lives and believes in me will never die" (John 11:25-26 NIV).

Existence does not end upon the death of the physical body. The spiritual entity stands before God. He is not the God of memories. All paths ultimately lead to God. When the physical body dies, you will stand before him for judgment and if you have believed, as he has said, you will never die.

"But God demonstrates his own love for us in this: while we were still sinners, Christ died for us" (Romans 5:8 NIV).

"For God so loved the world that he gave his one and only son, that whoever believes in him shall not perish, but have eternal life. For God did not send his Son into the world to condemn the world, but to save the world through him" (John 3:16-17 NIV).

God loved the world so much that he gave a part of the Trinity, God the son, not for condemnation of the world but the offering of life eternal for all who believe.

"I am the way and the truth and the life. No one comes to the Father except through me. If you really knew me, you would know my Father as well. From now on you do know him and have seen him" (John 14:6-7 NIV).

"For there is one God and one mediator between God and men, the man Christ Jesus, who gave himself as a ransom for all men—the testimony given in its proper time" 1 Timothy 2:5 NIV).

"Turn to me and be saved, all you ends of the earth; for I am God, and there is no other. By myself, I have sworn, my mouth has uttered in all integrity a word that will not be revoked: Before me every knee will bow; by me every tongue will swear" (Isaiah 45:22-23 NIV).

The only way to God the Father is through Jesus, God the son. There is no other way. If you find God the Son, you will find also God the Father, for they exist together.

"Believe me when I say that I am in the Father and the Father is in me" (John 14:11 NIV).

Solomon kept it straight and to the point when he said, "There is not a righteous man on earth who does what is right and never sins" (Ecclesiastes 7:20 NIV).

However, in the following Paul was much more detailed.

"Now we know that whatever the law says, it says to those who are under the law, so that every mouth may be silenced and the whole world held accountable to God. Therefore no one will be declared righteous in his sight for observing the law; rather through the law we become conscious of sin. But now a righteousness from God, apart from the law has been made known, to which the law and the prophets testify. This righteousness from God comes through faith in Jesus Christ to all who believe. There is no difference, for all have sinned and fall short of the glory of God, and are justified freely by his grace through the redemption that came by Christ Jesus. God presented him as a sacrifice of atonement, through faith in his blood" (Romans 3:19-25 NIV).

Christ supersedes or takes the place of the law because we cannot live by the law (Romans 10:14). One evil thought or deed and we would be lost for God demands perfection, but we cannot be perfect. Therefore, God accepted his son as a sacrifice for our sins so that we could be accepted as righteous in His sight. This also did away with the offerings by priests that were required on a regular basis under the law to cover ongoing sins; for the blood of Christ through the grace of God covers our sins once and for all.

While we can never understand the true wonderment of what was done for us, the following might help our comprehension: "Therefore when Christ came into the world, he said, 'Sacrifice and offering you did not desire, but a body you prepared for me; with burnt offerings and sin offerings you were not pleased.' Then I said, 'Here I am—it is written about me in the scroll—I have come down to do your will, O God" (Hebrews 10:5-7 NIV).

"He was delivered over to death for our sins and was raised to life for our justification" (Romans 4:25 NIV).

God's law speaks to all mankind. All have sinned. No one is perfect. Trying to follow the law does not make us righteous, but makes us aware of sin. Only faith in Jesus makes us righteous in God's sight.

"If you confess with your mouth Jesus is Lord, and believe in your heart that God raised him from the dead, you will be saved. For it is with your heart that you believe and are justified, and it is with your mouth that you confess and are saved" (Romans 10:9-10 NIV).

Christ supersedes the law. We only need to confess he is our Lord, and believe he rose from death, and in God's sight, we are justified. We will never be perfect while in the physical realm, but if we are sincere in our request for salvation, with each passing day we grow stronger.

"For it is by grace you have been saved through faith—and this is not from yourselves, it is the gift of God—not by works, so that no one can boast" (Ephesians 2:8 NIV).

"Blessed is he whose transgressions are forgiven; whose sins are covered. Blessed is the man whose sin the Lord does not count against him and in whose spirit is no deceit" (Psalm 32:1-2 NIV).

Show faith, ask for forgiveness, and forgiveness will be given. Our justification has nothing to do with anything we might have done, or anything we could ever do. It is a gift, free from God.

"For we are God's workmanship, created in Christ Jesus to do good works, which God created in advance for us to do" (Ephesians 2:10 NIV).

Created in Christ, good works were prepared in advance for his followers. Some will see immediate results from their works. Others might not ever realize what they have accomplished. A simple act of kindness, or a few well-placed words spoken in earnest, might start a chain reaction of events whose results won't be understood for several years. Be assured, the events and results fit perfectly with God's plan for he is in complete control.

"Love must be sincere. Hate what is evil; cling to what is good" (Romans 12:9 NIV).

Love what you know is pure and good. Do all within your power to preserve it. Keep as far as possible from what you perceive as evil. Ask for and rely on God's help.

"Live in harmony with one another" (Romans 12:16 NIV).

"Do not be overcome by evil, but overcome evil with good" (Romans 12:21 NIV).

The goodness and love that comes from God will eventually overcome all evil, and Christians should use this as their guide.

However, we have the God-given right to defend ourselves, our loved ones, and our nation from serious threats by any means necessary. For all other matters, trying to move forward in peace and harmony in accomplishing what is right by doing good is God's way.

Jesus' disciples asked him what they should do to do God's work (John 6:28 NIV). His answer was "the work of God is this: to believe in the one he has sent" (John 6:29 NIV). Jesus knew once they believed, all else would follow.

The disciples then asked for a miraculous sign similar to their forefathers receiving manna from heaven so they might see and believe (John 6:30-31 NIV). After telling them he was the true bread from heaven, Jesus declared: "I am the bread of life. He who comes to me will never go hungry, and he who believes in me will never be thirsty" (John 6:35 NIV).

"Who of you by worrying can add a single hour to his life? Since you cannot do this very little thing, why do you worry about the rest? Consider how the lilies grow. They do not labor or spin. Yet I tell you, not even Solomon in all his splendor was dressed like one of these. If that is how God clothes the grass of the field, which is here today, and tomorrow is thrown into the fire, how much more will he clothe you, O you of little faith!" (Luke 12:25-27 NIV).

God wants us to depend on him for all our needs. He is much more than a mere observer who might feel genuine compassion but be unable to help. He is the one who controls the course of events in our lives, and can bring all things together for good.

Controlling the Tongue

AT TIMES, IT is very difficult to control what we say. According to James 3:2 (NIV), "If anyone is never at fault in what he says, he is a perfect man, able to keep his whole body in check." James said this tongue in cheek. Since there was only one perfect man, Jesus, we realize no one has complete control over what comes out of his mouth. We can only strive to grow stronger in this area as we continue our journey with Christ.

"Likewise, the tongue is a small part of the body, but it makes great boasts. Consider what a great forest is set on fire by a small spark. The tongue also is like a fire, a world of evil among the parts of the body" (James 3:5-6 NIV).

"With the tongue we praise our Lord and father, and with it we curse men, who have been made in God's likeness. Out of the same mouth comes praise and cursing" (James 3:9-19 NIV).

The Parable of the Rich Fool

"**A MAN'S LIFE** does not consist in the abundance of his possessions" (Luke 12:15 NIV).

"What good is it for a man to gain the whole world, yet forfeit his soul? Or what can a man give in exchange for his soul?" (Mark 8:36-37 NIV).

The ground of a rich man did well, so much so he had no place to store his crops. He decided to tear down his storage area and build more and bigger ones to store all of his grain and goods. Then, his plan was to take life easy, eat, drink, and be merry. But in Luke 12, God said to him, "You fool! This very night your life will be demanded from you. Then who will get what you have prepared for yourself?" When telling this parable Jesus said, "This is how it will be with anyone who stores up things for himself but is not rich towards God" (Luke 12:16-21 NIV).

The foolish rich man thought only about himself and his possessions. He did not think about the fact that everything he possessed, including his physical life, was temporary. He failed to realize he should have stored his treasures, by helping others, in the vault of heaven where they would have lasted for eternity.

Once, when Jesus was having dinner at a tax collector's house with many more tax collectors and others who were considered sinners present, the teachers of the law asked why he was associating with sinners (Mark 2:15-16 NIV). His answer was, "It is not the healthy who need a doctor, but the sick. I have not come to call the righteous, but sinners" (Mark 2:17 NIV). What the self-righteous teachers of the law did not realize was they also needed his saving grace.

"One man considers one day more sacred than another; another man considers every day alike. Each one should be fully convinced in his own mind. He who regards one day as special, does so to the Lord" (Romans 14:5-6 NIV).

One believer should not pass judgment on another believer over disputable matters. Each need only be assured in their own mind they are doing what they think is best in their worship of God. If a person believes they are doing wrong, they are truly sinning.

"No eye has seen, no ear has heard, no mind has conceived what God has prepared for those who love him, but God has revealed it to us by his spirit" (1 Corinthians 2:9-10 NIV).

What God has prepared for us is revealed in part until we stand before Christ and the mist clears. As the following verse says: "Now we see but a poor reflection as in a mirror; then we shall see face to face. Now I know in part; then I shall know fully, even as I am fully known.

And now these three remain: faith, hope, and love. But the greatest of these is love" (1 Corinthians 13:12-13 NIV).

Many Jewish laws were condensed into the Ten Commandments. In effect, Jesus further reduced them to only two when He said, "Love the Lord your God with all your heart and with all your soul and with all your mind. This is the first and greatest commandment. And the second is like it: Love your neighbor as yourself. All the laws and the Prophets hang on these two commandments" (Matthew 22:37-40 NIV). And in Luke chapter 10 when Jesus told the parable of the Good Samaritan, He was saying in effect that everyone we meet is our neighbor.

Jesus also said, "A new commandment I give you: Love one another. As I have loved you, so you must love one another. By this all men will know that you are my disciples, if you love one another" (John 13:34-35 NIV).

And Paul's beautiful passage: "Love is patient, love is kind. It does not envy, it does not boast, it is not proud. It is not rude, it is not self-seeking, it is not easily angered, it keeps no record of wrongs. Love does not delight in evil but rejoices with the truth. It always protects, always trusts, always hopes, always perseveres" (1 Corinthians 13:4-7 NIV).

God's plan is headed toward one ultimate conclusion—love.

"So we fix our eyes not on what is seen, but on what is unseen. For what is seen is temporary, but what is unseen is eternal" (2 Corinthians 4:18 NIV).

While problems of the world are constantly pulling us down, they provide reasons for us to rely solely on God. We grow stronger spiritually by focusing on the unseen world which lasts for all eternity, instead of what is before us now, which lasts for a short time and then is no more.

The world and its desires pass away, but the man who does the will of God lives forever" (1 John 2:17 NIV).

There is one God, the Trinity. The only pathway between God and humanity is Jesus, God the son. He was born as a human, lived to manhood living a perfect, sin-free life, then allowed himself to be nailed to a cross and lifted from the ground as a sacrificial offering for the sins of all who would believe.

Then Peter began to speak: "I now realize how true it is that God does not show favoritism, but accepts men from every nation who fear him and do what is right" (Acts 10:34-35 NIV).

"From one man he made every nation of men, that they should inhabit the whole earth and he determined the times set for them and the exact places where they should live" (Acts 17:26 NIV).

"For there is no difference between Jew and Gentile—the same Lord is Lord of all and richly blesses all who call on him, for 'Everyone who calls on the name of the Lord will be saved" (Romans 10: 12-13 NIV).

Mankind is one race created in God's image. In His eyes, we are all equal.

"Blessed are the poor in spirit, for theirs is the kingdom of heaven" (Matthew 5:3 NIV).

As interpreted by The Message "You're blessed when you're at the end of your rope. With less of you, there is more of God and his rule."

Whenever self, the main obstacle between God and man, is taken from the equation, God's power becomes stronger, and he is better able to perform his works.

A Child is Born
A Son is Given

"COME TO ME, all you who are weary and burdened, and I will give you rest. Take my yoke upon you and learn from me, for I am gentle and humble in heart, and you will find rest for your souls. For my yoke is easy and my burden is light" (Matthew 11:28-30 NIV).

Jesus reveals his real personality—gentle and humble. All believers will truly find peace and meaning when they stand before him.

"For to us a child is born, to us a Son is given, and the government will be on his shoulders. And he will be called Wonderful Counselor, Mighty God, Everlasting Father, Prince of Peace. Of the increase of his government and peace there will be no end" (Isaiah 9:6-7 NIV).

A child is born resulting in the sacrifice of a son who will return and rule all governments of the world bringing never-ending peace and justice for all people.

"In my vision at night I looked, and there before me

was a son of man coming with the clouds of heaven. He approached the Ancient of Days and was led into his presence. He was given authority, glory and sovereign power; all peoples, nations and men of every language worshiped him. His dominion is an everlasting dominion that will not pass away, and his kingdom is one that will never be destroyed" (Daniel 7:13-14 NIV).

Daniel, the great interpreter of dreams, had a vision that foretold the coming of Christ. However, He will not return as the Sacrificial Lamb of God but as the sovereign ruler of the world bringing all peoples together as God's will is done on earth as it is in heaven.

Beautiful Words, Wonderful Promise, Dreadful Warning, Wisdom Speaks

"I LOVE THOSE who love me, and those who seek me find me" (Proverbs 8:17 NIV).

God is love. If you seek Him, you will find Him.

"The Lord brought me forth as the first of his works, before his deeds of old; I was appointed from eternity, from the beginning, before the world began" (Proverbs 8:22-23 NIV).

Anything beyond this point is irrelevant to mankind. No reason for speculation.

"Then I was the craftsman at his side. I was filled with delight day after day, rejoicing always in his presence, rejoicing in his whole world and delighting in mankind. Now then, my sons, listen to me; blessed are those who keep my ways" (Proverbs 8:30-32 NIV).

Everything was made through Jesus. All who accept Him as Lord of their lives are blessed.

"For whoever finds me finds life and receives favor from the Lord. But whoever fails to find me harms himself; all who hate me love death" (Proverbs 8:33-36 NIV).

It is very difficult understanding anyone hating God. But, there are many who prefer being their own god and establishing their own morals and codes of conduct.

Much is happening in America and throughout the world. Much of it is evil for Satan is still roaming through the earth and going back and forth in it (Job 1:7 NIV). The fall of humankind would not have happened if God had programmed us as robots to do His bidding. Instead, He gave us free will resulting in the ability for humankind to make its own choices. God wants our love for Him and worship of Him to be truly from us.

However, much of humanity is searching for answers everywhere but where the answers lie. Finding Jesus is the single most important aspect of our existence for: "The world and its desires pass away, but the person who does the will of God lives forever" (1 John 2:17 NIV). The following explains why evil, foolishness, and lack of common sense abounds within America and throughout the world—"The man without the Spirit does not accept the things that come from the Spirit of God, for they are foolishness to him, and he cannot understand them because they are spiritually discerned." (1 Corinthians 2:14 NIV). Believers have received God the Holy Spirit and through the Holy Spirit understand the gift of salvation and the ways of God. Those who do not believe, have within them the spirit of the world and cannot understand God's holy ways.

Abraham Lincoln said, "America will never be destroyed from the outside. If we falter and lose our freedom it will be because we destroyed ourselves." Sadly, it seems this very thing could happen. Political agendas, wealth, and power seem to be the god of many powerful people. An example is the issue of global warming. What does the Bible say? "As long as the earth endures, seedtime and harvest, cold and heat, summer and winter, day and night will never cease" (Genesis 8:22 NIV). Also the power-hungry greed that led to globalism has done much harm to America. As I write these words, there is widespread fear because of the coronavirus. And there is civil unrest across America which has led to protests and riots. Turn to the Word of God and you will find—"Do not follow the crowd in doing wrong" (Exodus 23:2 NIV).

In Luke, there is a beautiful imagery that shows God's love for Israel. "O Jerusalem, Jerusalem, you who kill the prophets and stone those sent to you, how often I have longed to gather your children together, as a hen gathers her chicks under her wings, but you were not willing" (Luke 13:34 NIV).

God feels the same toward all people because of His great love. If only we could abide by the following words from so many years ago—"If my people who are called by my name will humble themselves and pray and seek my face and turn from their wicked ways, then will I hear from heaven and will forgive their sins and will heal their land" (2 Chronicles 7:14 NIV).

In Revelation, Jesus is depicted as returning to earth riding a white horse followed by the armies of heaven also riding white horses (Rev. 19:11-14). Is this also beautiful imagery? It matters not. What matters is that He will return, and it will be in accordance with the will of God the Father.

A dim-lit room, a bed within a hospital. A person, ravaged by disease, a believer and follower of Christ. As the believer lay on what they knew was to be their deathbed, memories of their life flowed freely.

The most significant, the drawing power of God. Always relentless, always there, seeking entry into the depths of their soul. And God had succeeded in his quest, for they had accepted Christ as their Lord and Savior. As they lay, doubts crept in. The person knew they had not been perfect in the Christian life, but had grown stronger in Christ with the passing of time. The very character of their being had changed.

Suddenly they felt a presence, a presence of peace and comfort. Scripture flowed through their mind. "For it is by grace you have been saved, through faith and this is not from yourselves, it is the gift of God" (Ephesians 2:8 NIV). The presence grew stronger. Love filled the room. The person knew their physical body was dying to their spirit would soon stand before God. They would kneel and praise their Lord and then transcend into life eternal.

THE UNFORGIVABLE SIN

"**I TELL YOU** the truth, all the sins and blasphemies of men will be forgiven them. But whoever blasphemes against the Holy Spirit will never be forgiven; he is guilty of an eternal sin," (Mark 3:28-29).

There is no sin that will not be forgiven by God's grace except the sin of not accepting God the Holy Spirit. The individual who refuses to allow God's spirit to reside within has severed all ties with God and has no hope of salvation.

A dim-lit room, a bed within a hospital. A person, ravaged by disease; an atheist, not believing in God, His righteousness, or the need for salvation. As the atheist lay on what they knew was to be their deathbed, memories of their life flowed freely.

The most significant, the drawing power of the world. Always relentless, always there, seeking entry into the depth of their soul. And the world had succeeded in its quest, for they had accepted its ways, established their own morals, and become their own God. As they lay, doubts crept in. The person had focused little on this moment, quickly pushing it aside whenever it surfaced, continuing to live for the moment. Through pride and arrogance, they had developed a hatred for the very thought of God.

Suddenly, they felt a presence, an unfamiliar feeling of peace and comfort. An image appeared before them, a man with outstretched arms and love-filled eyes. Anger welled up inside the atheist, for they realized even though they had denied this man their entire life they were still being offered life eternal. Love of self and stubborn pride turned their heart to stone. The image slowly faded. The person thought they saw a tear fall from the man before the image vanished completely.

Coldness filled the room. Scripture flowed through their mind. "For whoever finds me finds life and receives favor from the Lord. But whoever fails to find me harms himself; all who hate me love death" (Proverbs 8:35-36 NIV). The person knew their physical body was dying and their spirit would soon stand before God. They would kneel before God and then face judgment.

Hebrews 2:6-9 NIV

"What is man that you are mindful of him, the son of man that you care for him? You made him a little lower than the angels; you crowned him with glory and honor and put everything under his feet.

In putting everything under mankind, God left nothing that is not subject to him. Yet at present we do not see everything subject to him. But we see Jesus, who was made a little lower than the angels, now crowned with glory and honor because he suffered death, so that by the grace of God he might taste death for everyone."

ROMANS 11:33-36 NIV (DOXOLOGY)

"Oh, the depth of the riches of the wisdom and knowledge of God! How unsearchable his judgments, and his paths beyond tracing out! Who has known the mind of the Lord! Or who has been his counselor? Who is ever given to God that God should repay him? For from him and through him and to him are all things. To him be the glory forever! Amen."

JUDE 1:24-25 NIV DOXOLOGY

"To him who is able to keep you from falling and to present you before his glorious presence without fault and with great joy—to the only God our Savior be glory, majesty, power and authority, through Jesus Christ our Lord, before all ages, now and foerevermore!" Amen.

I leave you with two thoughts. First, consider these words from the Psalmist, David. "Search me, O God, and know my heart; test me and know my anxious thoughts. See if there is any offensive way in me and lead me in the way everlasting" (Psalm 139:23-24 NIV).

Secondly, if you have not yet accepted Jesus as your Savior and Lord, perhaps it is time to revisit Romans

10:9-10. "If you confess with your mouth Jesus is Lord, and believe in your heart that God raised him from the dead, you will be saved. For it is with your heart that you believe and are justified, and it is with your mouth that you confess and are saved."

God bless,

Burl L. Shepard

www.ingramcontent.com/pod-product-compliance
Lightning Source LLC
LaVergne TN
LVHW090039080526
838202LV00046B/3877